SPORTS
ALL-ST★RS

NAOMI OSAKA

Jon M. Fishman

Lerner Publications ◆ Minneapolis

Lerner Publications Company
An imprint of Lerner Publishing Group, Inc.
241 First Avenue North
Minneapolis, MN 55401 USA

For reading levels and more information, look up this title at www.lernerbooks.com.

Main body text set in Albany Std. Typeface provided by Agfa.

Editor: Shee Yang
Lerner team: Sue Marquis

Library of Congress Cataloging-in-Publication Data

Names: Fishman, Jon M., author.
Title: Naomi Osaka / Jon M. Fishman.
Description: Minneapolis, MN : Lerner Publications, [2021] | Series: Sports all-stars (Lerner sports) | Includes bibliographical references and index. | Audience: Ages 7–11 | Audience: Grades 2–3 | Summary: "Born in the US, raised in a Haitian and Japanese household, and known for her tennis talent, Naomi Osaka is the first Asian player to hold the top ranking for singles tennis. Learn her story!"— Provided by publisher.
Identifiers: LCCN 2019053396 (print) | LCCN 2019053397 (ebook) | ISBN 9781541597518 (library binding) | ISBN 9781728414058 (paperback) | ISBN 9781728401003 (ebook)
Subjects: LCSH: Osaka, Naomi, 1997—-Juvenile literature. | Women tennis players—Japan—Biography—Juvenile literature. | Women tennis players—United States—Biography—Juvenile literature.
Classification: LCC GV994.O73 F57 2021 (print) | LCC GV994.O73 (ebook) | DDC 796.342092 [B]—dc23

LC record available at https://lccn.loc.gov/2019053396
LC ebook record available at https://lccn.loc.gov/2019053397

Manufactured in the United States of America
1-47855-48295-9/16/2020

CONTENTS

Naomi Osaka sends a serve to her opponent during the 2019 Australian Open.

Whack! Naomi Osaka's tennis racket smacked the ball and sent it zooming into the net. It was her second missed **serve** in a row. The **double fault** gave a point to her opponent, Ashleigh Barty. Osaka lost the first **set**, 3–6.

- **Date of Birth:** October 16, 1997

- **Position:** singles tennis player

- **League: Women's Tennis Association (WTA)**

- **Professional highlights:** became a pro tennis player at the age of 14; won the 2018 US Open; won the 2019 Australian Open; won the 2019 China Open

- **Personal highlights:** was born in Osaka, Japan; began playing tennis at the age of three; loves to shop for clothes and play video games

Osaka and Barty share a handshake after Osaka's incredible win at the 2019 Australian Open.

Osaka and Barty were playing at the China Open in October 2019. The tournament in Beijing, China, is a Women's Tennis Association event. Barty was the world's top singles player in the WTA rankings. Osaka was ranked fourth.

Osaka took a 3–2 lead in the second set. Barty served, and Osaka took a fierce **backhand** swing. The ball sailed past Barty to give Osaka a point. When Barty hit the ball out of bounds a few moments later, Osaka won the game. She kept winning and took the set 6–3.

Barty served first in the third and final set. Osaka stayed back from the net to make sure Barty couldn't easily blast a shot past her. The tennis superstars smacked the ball back and forth over and over again. The set stayed even.

Finally, Barty began hitting the ball out of bounds and into the net. Osaka took the third set 6–2 to win the China Open. She received a huge trophy and more than $1.5 million in prize money.

For much of 2019, Osaka had struggled to win. Winning in China was proof that she was back and better than ever. "I really wanted to win here, I felt like I had something to prove," she said.

Osaka holds up the 2019 China Open trophy during the award ceremony.

Osaka prepares to return a shot on day one of the Bank of the West Classic on July 28, 2014.

Leonard Francois grew up in Haiti and attended college in New York. Around 1990, he went to study in Japan. That's where he met Tamaki Osaka and fell in love. On October 16, 1997,

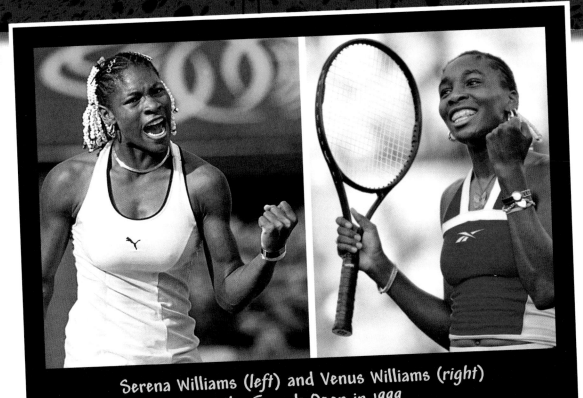

Serena Williams (*left*) and Venus Williams (*right*)
at the French Open in 1999

Naomi was born in Osaka, Japan. Her sister, Mari, had been born 18 months earlier.

In 1999, Francois watched on TV as Venus and Serena Williams played tennis at the French Open. Their story was famous. Venus and Serena's father had never played pro tennis. But starting when his daughters were young, he pushed and trained them to play. By 1999, they were two of the best players in the world.

The success of the Williams family inspired Francois. He wanted Naomi and Mari to become as successful as Venus and Serena. As part of his plan, the family moved to New York when Naomi was three. Right away, Francois started tennis lessons with the girls.

Naomi and Mari trained together on **public** tennis courts. As they grew stronger, Francois pushed them harder. Each sister took thousands of practice swings a day. The sisters also played against each other. But the 18-month age difference was too much for Naomi to overcome. She always lost, often without winning a single set. "Every day I'd say, 'I'm going to beat you tomorrow,'" Naomi said. Trying to top her sister helped Naomi get better. It would take 12 years before she could defeat Mari.

In New York, Naomi and her family lived with her father's parents. At home, the family spoke English, Japanese, and Creole. Creole is a French-based language spoken by some people in Haiti.

Osaka (*second from left*) and her family pose for a photo with the president of Haiti, Jovenel Moise (*center left*), and First Lady, Martine Etienne Joseph (*center right*), in Haiti on November 8, 2018.

In 2006, Francois decided it was time to focus on tennis full-time. The family moved again, this time to Pembroke Pines, Florida. Florida's warm weather allowed Naomi and Mari to play outside all year. Francois and Tamaki also began to **homeschool** their daughters, giving them even more time for tennis.

The family's focus on tennis paid off. In 2013, Naomi became a pro player at the age of 14. But as a newcomer to pro tennis, it would take her years to climb to the top of the WTA rankings. First, she had to train like a world-class athlete.

Osaka during practice on June 16, 2019, after qualifying for the Nature Valley Classic

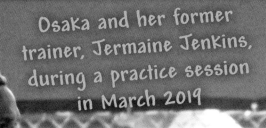

Osaka and her former trainer, Jermaine Jenkins, during a practice session in March 2019

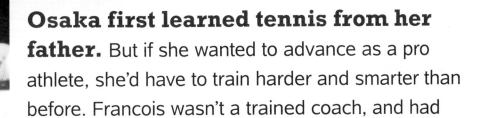

Osaka first learned tennis from her father. But if she wanted to advance as a pro athlete, she'd have to train harder and smarter than before. Francois wasn't a trained coach, and had never played pro tennis. Osaka needed expert training that her father could not provide. In 2013, she began working with new coaches.

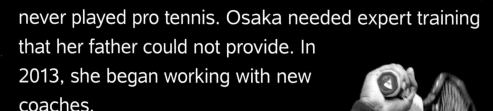

With her coaches and a practice partner, Osaka works on every aspect of her game. She takes thousands of swings a day, just as she did as a child. Osaka warms up on court by hitting short shots over the net to a partner. Soon the players back up and begin hitting the ball with longer and harder strokes.

Next, Osaka practices her serve. If her partner can hit it back, they play until someone wins the point. Osaka talks to her coach about how she's playing. Then she serves again.

During practice, Osaka faces different types of tennis shots. Her partner hits fast serves and high, slow **lobs**. He hits balls quickly from close range. Osaka sends all of them streaking back over the net.

Osaka training for the 2020 Fed Cup Qualifier on February 6, 2020

Osaka returns a shot in the second round of the 2020 Australian Open

The average WTA match lasts more than 90 minutes. Some are longer than three hours. To make sure she can keep playing hard no matter how long a match lasts, Osaka works with a fitness coach.

A WTA **rally** usually ends in just a few seconds. With her fitness coach, Osaka practices intense rallies that last three minutes. As time passes, her heart pounds and her legs burn. She fights the pain and concentrates on hitting good shots.

Osaka also uses special gear to strengthen her muscles. With a resistance band around her legs, she throws a heavy ball back and forth with her coach. As they throw, Osaka moves sideways across the court. She stretches the band with each step, strengthening her legs and helping her move quickly from side to side during matches.

Osaka works with two trainers to improve her focus while also building leg strength.

Osaka whacks the ball to her opponent and idol Serena Williams during the 2018 US Open final.

Osaka celebrates a good shot during the 2018 US Open.

Osaka's WTA breakthrough came at the 2018 US Open. She entered the tournament as the 20th-ranked player. But no one could keep up with her strength and power. She faced Serena Williams in the final match and won both sets. Osaka lost just one set during the tournament.

In the 2018 US Open final, Osaka hit a serve 119 miles (191 km) per hour. It was the fastest serve of the match. Her average serve speed was 109 miles (175 km) per hour.

Winning the US Open skyrocketed Osaka's popularity around the world. A watch she wore during the tournament almost sold out in stores. Even the type of strings she used in her tennis rackets began to sell better.

Companies took notice of Osaka's popularity. Her image appeared on products such as instant noodles. She signed deals to **endorse** products for Nike, Mastercard, and others. In 2019, *Forbes* magazine said Osaka was the second-highest-paid female athlete in the world.

Osaka has fun with her money. "Every day is like Christmas," Mari says of her sister's recent spending habits. Osaka especially loves to buy clothes and stay on top of fashion. She says that music superstar Rihanna is her fashion role model.

Osaka poses alongside a poster of her for the skin care brand Shiseido on October 28, 2019, in Shenzhen, China.

Osaka also likes to attend concerts and other public events. But she's still getting used to her status as a celebrity. She gets recognized wherever she goes. In Japan, she sometimes has to sneak into her hotel to avoid fans and reporters.

Osaka signs autographs for fans at the Toray Pan Pacific Open on September 22, 2019.

Gamer

Traveling the world for tennis tournaments includes a lot of time waiting around in hotels. Osaka fills some of her downtime with video games. She travels with her console to play games such as *Overwatch*.

Osaka loves video games so much that she sometimes borrows from them to express herself. In 2016, a reporter asked her what her goals were. "To be the very best, like no one ever was," Osaka said. The reporter didn't recognize the expression. "I'm sorry," Osaka said. "That's the *Pokémon* theme song."

Osaka takes a selfie with fans after winning a match during the 2019 US Open.

GLOBAL SUPERSTAR

Osaka competes at the 2019 Australian Open.

About five months after winning the US Open, Osaka entered the 2019 Australian Open. She was the tournament's fourth-ranked player. Fans expected her to do well, and she didn't disappoint them.

The sun sets over Osaka and Kvitova's finals match during the 2019 Australian Open.

Osaka reached the championship match against eighth-ranked Petra Kvitova. Both players fought hard for the title. Osaka won the first set by one game, and Kvitova took the second by two games.

In the third set, Osaka served with a chance to win the match. She swung and sent the ball zooming at 113 miles (182 km) per hour. Kvitova couldn't reach it. Osaka was the 2019 Australian Open champion!

After she won in Australia, the WTA ranked Osaka the world's top female tennis player. She is the first person from Asia to rank at the top of the men's or women's rankings. But she didn't stay there for long. She failed to win another tournament for almost eight months.

In September 2019, Osaka won the Pan Pacific Open in Osaka, Japan, the city where she was born. The next month she won the China Open, her second victory in a row. Naomi Osaka was back.

In 2019, *Time* named Osaka one of the 100 Most Influential People in the world. The list includes famous artists, world leaders, and athletes.

At the 2020 US Open in September, Osaka made it to the final. She faced Victoria Azarenka, the 27th-ranked player in the world. Osaka beat Azarenka in three sets to win the tournament for the second time.

Osaka decided to play for Japan at the next Olympic Games. The Olympics will take place in Tokyo, Japan. "It is a special feeling to aim for the Olympics as a representative of Japan," she said. "I think it will be more emotional to play for the pride of the country." Whether she's playing for her country or herself, Osaka will keep fighting to be the world's best tennis player.

Osaka plans to win many more tennis trophies in the future.

All-Star Stats

A huge serve is a big advantage in tennis. Starting play with a fierce blast is a good way to keep your opponent off balance. Luckily for Osaka, she has one of the best serves ever. Take a look at the fastest serves in WTA history.

Player	Serve speed in miles (km) per hour
1. Sabine Lisicki	131 (210.8)
2. Venus Williams	129 (207.6)
3. Serena Williams	128.6 (206.9)
4. Julia Goerges	126.1 (202.9)
5. Brenda Schultz-McCarthy	126 (202.7)
6. Nadiia Kichenok	125.5 (201.9)
7. Naomi Osaka	125 (201.1)
Lucie Hradecka	125
Anna-Lena Groenefeld	125
9. Ana Ivanovic	124.9 (201)
Denisa Allertova	124.9

Glossary

backhand: a stroke made with the back of the hand turned in the direction of movement

double fault: two missed serves in a row that result in the loss of a point

endorse: recommend a product or service, usually in exchange for money

homeschool: to teach school subjects to one's children at home

lobs: soft high-arching shots

public: accessible to all members of the community

rally: a series of shots between players before a point is won

serve: to hit the ball to begin play

set: a group of six or more games

Women's Tennis Association (WTA): the governing body of women's pro tennis

Source Notes

7 "'My Attitude Was Trash': Naomi Osaka Beats Barty in China Open Final," *Guardian (US edition)*, October 6, 2019, https://www.theguardian.com/sport/2019/oct /06/attitude-trash-naomi-osaka-ashleigh-barty-china -open-final-tennis.

10 Brook Larmer, "Naomi Osaka's Breakthrough Game," *New York Times*, August 23, 2018, https://www.nytimes .com/2018/08/23/magazine/naomi-osakas-breakthrough -game.html.

21 Sean Gregory, "Tennis Star Naomi Osaka Doesn't Like Attention. She's about to Get a Ton of It," *Time*, January 10, 2019, https://time.com/5498898/naomi-osaka/.

23 Antonia Noori Farzan, "Japanese, Haitian, and Now a Grand Slam Winner: Naomi Osaka's Historic Journey to the U.S. Open," *Washington Post*, September 10, 2018, https://www.washingtonpost.com/news/morning -mix/wp/2018/09/10/japanese-haitian-and-now-a-grand -slam-winner-naomi-osakas-historic-journey-to-the-u-s -open/.

27 David Wharton, "Tennis Star Naomi Osaka Chooses Japan over U.S. for 2020 Tokyo Olympics," *Los Angeles Times*, October 10, 2019, https://www.latimes.com/sports /olympics/story/2019-10-10/naomi-osaka-chooses-japan -over-u-s-2020-tokyo-olympics.

Braun, Eric. *Incredible Sports Trivia: Fun Facts and Quizzes*. Lerner Publications: Minneapolis, 2018.

Naomi Osaka Official Site
https://www.naomiosaka.com/en/profile/

Naomi Osaka—WTA Tennis
https://www.wtatennis.com/players/319998/naomi-osaka

Scheff, Matt. *Naomi Osaka*. Lake Elmo, MN: Focus Readers, 2020.

Smith, Elliott. *Serena Williams*. Minneapolis: Lerner Publications, 2021.

US Open
https://www.usopen.org/index.html

Index

Photo Acknowledgments

Image credits: LEO RAMIREZ/AFP/Getty Images, p. 4; GREG BAKER/AFP/Getty Images, p. 6; Cui Xinyu/Getty Images, p. 7; Ezra Shaw/Getty Images, p. 8; STAFF/AFP/Getty Images, p. 9; AP Photo/Dieu Nalio Chery, p. 11; Jordan Mansfield/Getty Images, p. 12; Kyodo News/Getty Images, pp. 13, 27; ASANKA BRENDON RATNAYAKE/AFP/Getty Images, p. 14; Jose Breton/Pics Action/NurPhoto/Getty Images, p. 15; Jason Heidrich/Icon Sportswire/Getty Images, p. 16; AP Photo/Andy Wong, p. 17; Tim Clayton - Corbis/Getty Images, pp. 18, 23; Mohammed Elshamy/Anadolu Agency/Getty Images, p. 19; VCG/Getty Images, p. 21; The Asahi Shimbun/Getty Images, p. 22; TPN/Getty Images, p. 24; Chaz Niell/Icon Sportswire/Getty Images, p. 25. Design element throughout: iconeer/iStock/Getty Images.

Cover: WANG ZHAO/AFP/Getty Images.